The Tale of the Holy Girl

Copyright © 2022 by Eric J. Epstein,

Illustration by Avjit Sil, all rights reserved.
No part of this publication may be reproduced, stored in a retrieval system or transmitted in any form or by any means (electronic, mechanical, photocopying, recording or otherwise) without prior written
permission of the author.

Printed in the United States of America

ISBN: 978-1-7350318-4-2

Once there was a family that lived in the woods. There was a mother, a father, a brother, and a sister as well as many animals. They enjoyed a simple life and were thankful that they had food to eat, a home to live in, and warm fires when it was cold.

They didn't have much money and often didn't see other people because they had so much work to do but this gave them a lot of time together and ensured conflicts did not linger.

One winter evening when all were resting inside after a day of taking care of their animals and repairing the barn, there was a knock at the door. "A visitor!," yelled the brother and he and his sister ran to the door. "Stop!," said Father, "We don't know who it is and I must make sure it's safe."

As Father opened the door, a small, old man stood shivering in the doorway wearing purple sackcloth clothes and boots. He talked with Father about being a monk who had traveled from far away and needing a place to warm himself for the next part of his journey. Father welcomed him inside to sit by the fire and meet the family. Mother brought him some food and drink and soon all were telling stories and laughing.

Sister noticed that the monk looked at her occasionally with a warm, kind look on his face. His eyes seemed so full and deep that she felt like she might fall into them. She also felt somehow special.

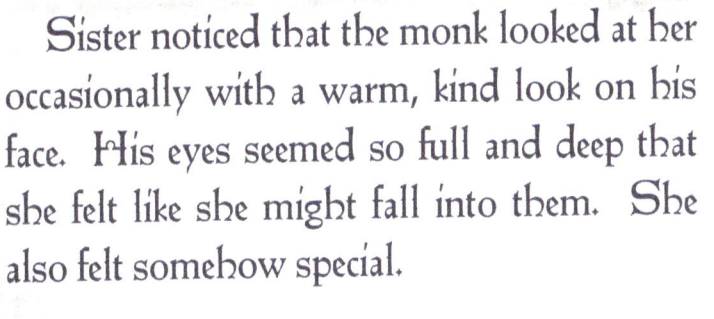

When it was time for bed and Father invited the monk to spend the night, he declined and said he needed to keep walking while the moon was bright.

However, the monk did ask if he could bless the sister because he believed that the sister was holy. Father and Mother were surprised but could see no wrong in the request.

The monk put both of his hands on Sister's shoulders and looked into her eyes. She wanted to look away but forced herself not to because she wanted to see everything that was happening. He said only one phrase, "May your heart always keep its strong feelings." Then the monk lifted his hands, smiled at all of the family and walked out the door.

Father and Mother were not sure what to make of this experience and talked about it into the night. Brother felt left out and did his best to tease Sister often before bed. It was decided that Father would go to town the next day and learn more about this monk and his blessings.

When Father arrived in town the next morning, he spoke to the wisest people he knew and no one could make sense of the experience. Everyone had different ideas about it, but all were very curious. Word traveled fast and soon the home was receiving many visitors who had come to meet the holy girl and receive some of her blessing. It was very tiring for the family because they rarely had time to get their work done and many visitors left gifts that were very impractical and distracting for the sister.

Problems seemed to follow for the sister in those days and she found herself sinking further and further into herself and away from others. If she talked to the visitors, they would often be grumpy with her for sounding so much like a little girl and not like some wise person. Some would try and make her words into wise sayings, even if she had not meant them that way.

Her brother was always frustrated with her and even her parents seemed weary of her never being available to do her jobs and always having so many worthless conversations and trinkets lying around.

Soon the Sister became nearly silent and found that she was angry at everyone. She felt that everyone was against her and her heart was filled with a deep sadness that she never showed as anything but anger. This only made things worse as her family assumed she was being prideful and her visitors believed she was even more wise in her silence and powerful in her anger. She thought with loathing at the monk's words about her "feelings always being strong" because all of her feelings seemed so horrible.

The family argued often and it seemed that the good old days when life was simple would never return. Then one evening, there was a knock on the door. Father didn't even stand up and said loudly that "there will be no more visitors today!"

In the morning when they all trudged outside to grumpily get some chores done before the people came, they noticed a note on the door.

Each family member was inwardly remorseful as their first feeling was of gladness that this man who had brought them so much sorrow was now gone. Father said that he would bring the family to town and hopefully bring an end to this mess.

> Your friend the monk has died and has left you a gift. Please meet me at the town hall tomorrow at noon.

At the town hall was a woman who looked slightly like the monk and smiled broadly at the weary Father and Sister. She stated that she was a part of a guild of women healers and learners who were always seeking new members. The monk had been a dear friend of theirs because he knew how to find girls who were often the wisest and most perceptive of their members.

His gift to the family was to recommend Sister into their guild and to pay for her entrance expenses.

Father and Sister listened to the woman but soon could not contain themselves any longer. "Why did he ruin our lives by saying that Sister was holy?"; "Why did he say I should keep my strong feelings when they have caused nothing but pain?"

The woman's face bowed in sorrow as she realized how heavily the misunderstanding had lain upon the family. "To be holy simply means to be set apart for a true purpose," she told them. "Although the monk happened to see a particular purpose in the girl's eyes, all people have a true purpose and so are holy. The monk only meant to encourage you through his blessing.

He wanted you to trust that your strong feelings were good when so many girls with strong feelings are made to think they are wrong to have them or that they have no purpose. Emotions are a way of knowing; they show how one is affected by the world. In doing so they show the deeper things of this world."

So this Holiness wasn't some kind of magic that others could get from me; just something we all have?," Sister asked.

The woman nodded, "This is true but few honor life and emotions as the holy gifts that they are. Purpose exists in all situations and people. Our painful emotions can show us that we need to look deeper for this purpose. Even when the neighbors treated you wrongly, it revealed what you truly value. You want to be known as a good part of your family and to be understood for who you really are."

As the weight of confusion lifted, they embraced the wise woman.

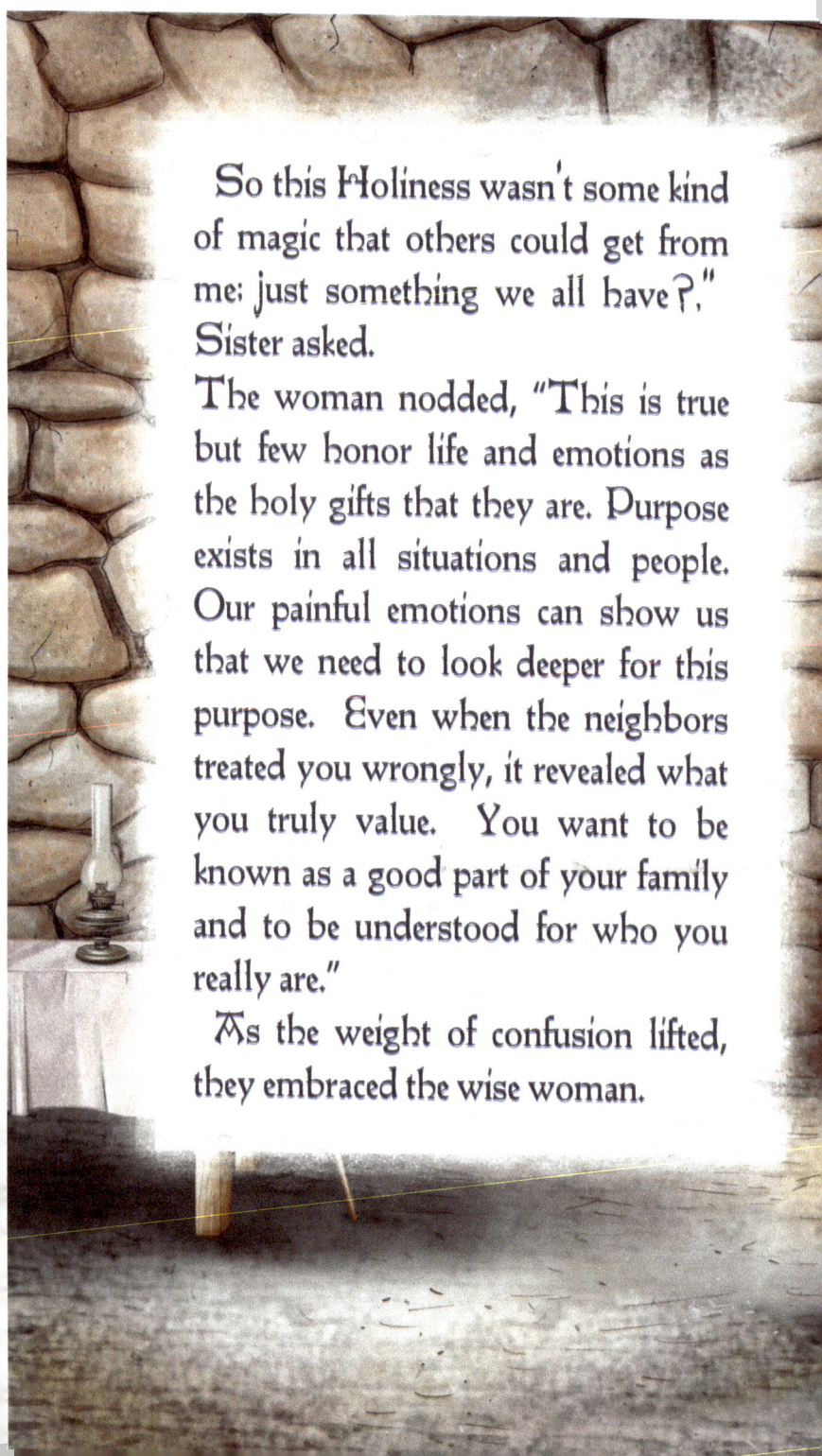

The family turned and looked at each other with new eyes. They were shocked by how such a small confusion could lead to such great harm. "Why were we so cruel to each other?," Father said quietly. The woman looked on him with compassion and understanding as if she had fallen into the same mistake once.

"Living with the belief that you are holy is the most dangerous way to live. It makes one more likely to suffer and more often affected by deception."

When they were all home and their story had been retold, Father immediately began work on a sign for the front of the house that read, "The holy girl is gone, but all are a part of a higher purpose."

www.ingramcontent.com/pod-product-compliance
Lightning Source LLC
Chambersburg PA
CBHW061742070526
44585CB00024B/2782